Plastic

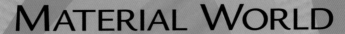
Plastic

by Claire Llewellyn

W
FRANKLIN WATTS
A Division of Scholastic Inc.
NEW YORK TORONTO LONDON AUCKLAND SYDNEY
MEXICO CITY NEW DELHI HONG KONG
DANBURY, CONNECTICUT

First published in 2002 by
Franklin Watts
96 Leonard Street
London EC2A 4XD

First American edition 2002 by Franklin Watts
A Division of Scholastic Inc.
90 Sherman Turnpike
Danbury, CT 06816

ISBN 0-531-14631-6 (lib. bdg.) 0-531-14838-6 (pbk.)

Catalog details are available from the
Library of Congress Cataloging-in-Publication data

Series Editor: Rosalind Beckman
Series Designer: James Evans
Picture Research: Diana Morris
Photography: Steve Shott

Printed in Hong Kong, China

Acknowledgments

Thanks are due to the following for kind permission to reproduce photographs:

James Davis Travel Photography: 16-17b. Julio Etchart/Still Pictures: 22r. Chris Fairclough/Franklin Watts: 7clb, 8t, 8b. Peter Frischmuth/Still Pictures: 27t. Pascal Goetgheluck/SPL: 19r. Nick Hanna/Eye Ubiquitous: 11t. Robert Harding PL: 14-15c. Images Colour Library: back cover. Helen Lisher/Eye Ubiquitous: 11c. Maximillian Stock Ltd/Robert Harding PL: 18b. Ray Moller/Franklin Watts: 7r, 9t. NASA/SPL: 21b. Stephen Rafferty/Eye Ubiquitous: 12l. Skjold/Eye Ubiquitous: 25t. Tek Image/SPL: 23t.

Thanks are also due to John Lewis and Vita Thermoplastic Compounds Ltd. for their help with this book.

Contents

Words printed in **_bold italic_** are explained in the glossary.

What Is Plastic?

Plastic is one of the most useful materials in the world. It is used to make thousands of different things. Look around and you will see plastic in homes, cars, hospitals, and schools. It is hard to imagine life without it.

All Sorts of Plastic

The name *plastic* is given to hundreds of very different materials. Some people use the word *plastics* instead. One kind of plastic often looks and feels different from another. Different plastics behave in different ways.

Made of Plastic

All the things in these pictures are made of plastic. Can you name them all?

KETCHUP

Material Words

Which of these words describes plastic?

cold   thick   shiny
sticky   stretchy
stiff   solid
heavy
soft   strong
dull
hard   warm
durable
spongy   light
crisp
colorful
rough   smooth
thin
flexible   slimy
springy
squashy

Fantastic Fact

The word *plastic* describes materials that can be bent or molded into shape. Plasticine is one of these.

Plastic Can Be Hard or Soft

Plastics are not all the same. Some of them are hard and strong. Others are squashy and soft. We use hard and soft kinds of plastic in very different ways.

Hard Plastics

Hard plastic can be shaped to make things like tables and chairs, garbage pails, and flower pots. This kind of plastic is very sturdy and always keeps its shape.

Garden equipment is often made of plastic. This is because plastic is strong and easy to clean.

Soft Plastics

Soft plastic is not as strong as hard plastic, and it does not keep its shape. It can be rolled or folded up small. This kind of plastic is used to make things like umbrellas and bags.

Try This

All the items in this picture are made of plastic. Some of them are hard. Others are soft. Can you put them in order from hardest to softest?

Plastic Is Light but Strong

Plastic can be very strong. Many strong materials, such as concrete or wood, are heavy. Plastic is not heavy. It is very light. This makes it especially useful.

A plastic basket is very light, but it can hold a lot of clothes.

Easier to Carry

Plastic bottles and tubes are used to carry all kinds of things, from milk and fruit juice to paint and shampoo. Plastic bottles are lighter than glass. This makes them easier to carry and cheaper to transport.

Plastic bottles are safer than glass. If you drop them, they will not break.

Lighter Than Before

Airplanes and cars were once made of heavy materials such as metal, leather, and wood. Now many of the parts are made of plastic instead. Cars and planes are much lighter, so they need less *energy* to move. This means that they burn a lot less fuel.

Inside a plane there are hundreds of different plastic parts.

Plastic parts are used all over a car, even in the trunk!

Try This

Plastic bags are light but strong. How many potatoes can you put in a bag before the handles stretch? How many can you put in before the handles break?

Plastic Is Clean and Durable

Plastic is useful in the home. It is easy to care for, lasts a long time, and comes in many different colors.

Easy Care

Some materials, such as wood or metal, need a lot of care. They need polishing, painting, cleaning, or oiling to keep them looking good. Plastic is much easier to keep looking new. It does not rust or break, and it is hard to mark or scratch.

Plastic window frames last longer than wood and do not need to be painted.

Lots of Wear

Think of all the household goods that are made of plastic: vacuum cleaners, kettles, cutting boards, food containers, and kitchen tools. Some of these things are washed every day. They all take very hard wear.

Fantastic Fact

False teeth are made of plastic. They are durable and easy to clean.

Plastic Is Waterproof

Plastic is a **waterproof** material. It does not let water or other liquids through. Plastic helps keep things dry and is very useful out of doors.

Keeps Out the Weather

Plastic is useful for outdoor equipment such as jungle gyms, wheelbarrows, and pipes. It lasts for many years because it does not rust or rot in wet weather. Plastic can also be made into waterproof cloth, which is great for rain gear. Rain runs off a plastic coat, so you stay dry.

Keeps Out the Wet

Some things spoil if they get wet, especially if they are made of paper. Look at the cover of this book. A thin layer of plastic protects it if it gets wet or dirty. At outdoor markets, plastic sheets provide a "roof" for stalls to protect goods and shoppers from the rain.

Foods spoil quickly in the rain. A plastic roof helps to protect them.

Try This

Find two pieces of wallpaper, one with a coating of plastic and one without. Each day, mark them with a washable felt pen. When the ink is dry, wipe them clean with a damp cloth. After a week, compare the two. What do you find?

Plastic Is Made from Oil

Plastic is not a **natural** material. It was invented by scientists. It is made from the **chemicals** in oil.

Inventing Plastics

Oil is a valuable material that is found deep inside the ground. When **crude oil** is taken to an **oil refinery**, most of it is used to make fuel. Some of the oil is used to make plastic. Scientists are always searching for new materials. By **experimenting** with different chemicals in oil, they have invented many different kinds of plastic.

Plastic is made from oil at huge factories called oil refineries.

From Oil to Granules

Sometimes powdered wood or clay is added to plastic. This makes a stronger or smoother material. Adding **dyes** produces plastic in many different colors. Oil refineries produce plastic in tiny **granules**, or chips. These are delivered to factories and turned into goods.

At the factory, the fine granules of plastic are made into many different products.

Fantastic Fact

It takes just two handfuls of plastic granules to make a washtub.

Plastic Is Easy to Shape

At the factory, the plastic is heated until it melts. It can then be shaped by different machines.

Molding Plastic

When the plastic granules are heated, they melt into a thick liquid. The runny plastic is squeezed, pressed, or blown into **molds**, where it quickly cools and hardens.

Molds are used to make all kinds of things, such as plastic bowls and toys.

Melted plastic looks like a thick, gooey syrup.

Squeezing and Fizzing

Melted plastic is shaped in other ways, too. Squeezing it through holes produces hollow tubes that can be turned into hoses, pipes, and bags. Fizzing gas into the melted plastic fills it with bubbles. This makes a light, very springy foam called *polystyrene*.

This machine is making plastic bags. A tube of soft plastic is filled with air before it is flattened and cut.

Try This

Examine two different things made of polystyrene. Why is this material so useful?

Plastic Can Be Made into Fibers

Soft plastic can be used to make *fibers*. The fibers are woven into many kinds of cloth that last well and are easy to care for.

Fine synthetic fibers are made into sewing thread.

Making the Fibers

When runny plastic is squirted through tiny holes, it makes long, thin plastic fibers. The fibers harden as they cool, and they can be used for weaving or knitting. Scientists have invented dozens of different fibers, such as nylon, *polyester*, and acrylic. These are called *synthetic* fibers.

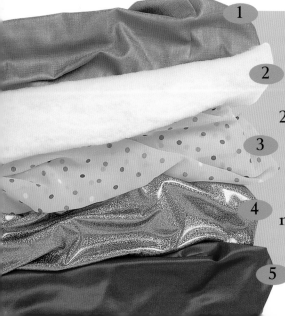

Polyester is one of the most popular synthetic fabrics.

1. This fabric has the uneven feel of linen.

2. Layers of fine polyester are used for filling quilts, cushions, and pillows.

3. This fine polyester has the look and feel of silk.

4. Polyester sparkles when it is woven with metal thread.

5. A shiny, smooth polyester looks like satin.

New Materials

Synthetic fibers are used in different ways. Some are good for making carpets and chairs because they are **fireproof** and do not show the dirt. Many other fibers are used to make clothes. Some of them are shiny like silk, or warm and fluffy like wool.

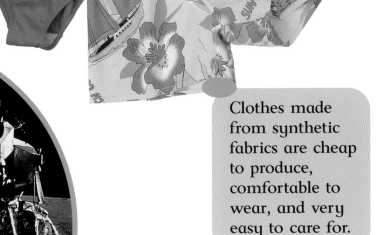

Clothes made from synthetic fabrics are cheap to produce, comfortable to wear, and very easy to care for.

Fantastic Fact

The flag on the Moon is made of nylon. Nylon was the first cloth ever to be made from plastic.

Plastic Makes Garbage

Plastic goods are hard to throw away. They do not rot and cannot be burned safely. Getting rid of plastic is a serious problem. It is one we have to try and solve.

Getting Rid of Plastic

It is hard to get rid of old plastic bottles and bags. Burying plastic waste does not work because it just stays in the ground. Burning plastic is dangerous. When it burns, it produces **gases** that poison and **pollute** the air. Plastic garbage is building up and causing problems for the **environment**.

Plastic waste looks ugly on the ground and will not rot away.

Too Many Landfills

In most towns, garbage is buried in *landfills*. These ugly, smelly places produce harmful gases and attract rats and other pests. Plastic waste takes up a lot of space. As we throw away more and more plastic, we will need more and more ugly landfill sites. We need to use plastic carefully and cut down on plastic waste.

Landfills are one way of getting rid of trash, but they also harm the environment.

Try This

Find a plastic cup and a paper cup and bury them under the ground. Remember to mark the spot. A few weeks later, dig up the cups and compare them. What do you notice?

Cutting Down on Plastic

As more goods are made out of plastic, more of them end up in the garbage. We need to use plastic more carefully so that there will be less of it to throw away.

Too Much Plastic

Throwing away plastic is a waste. It is not just a waste of the material itself. It is also a waste of the oil and energy that were used to produce it. We need to use plastic more carefully and save it whenever we can.

All plastic food containers end up as litter. Paper bags or boxes would be a better choice.

Some towns have plastic banks where waste plastic can be recycled.

Reusing Plastic

Saving plastic helps protect the environment. There are three ways of doing this. We can reduce the amount of plastic we use by cutting down on packaging. We can reuse some plastic products by using one good plastic bag instead of many cheaper ones. We can also **recycle** waste plastic by taking it to the plastic bank to be turned into recycled plastic.

Try This

If you eat a packed lunch, try to reuse the same box and bottle each day, instead of throwing them away when you have finished eating.

Recycling Plastic

Some plastic can be recycled and used to make new things. Recycling plastic is not easy. There are many different types of plastic, and each one needs to be recycled on its own.

Sorting Plastic

Plastic bottles are made of different kinds of plastic. Most of them are now marked with a code to show what kind of plastic it is. This helps people sort out their bottles ready for recycling. In some places, they can take them to plastic bottle banks.

All these bottles can be recycled and made into new plastic goods.

Plastic waste arrives at the factory for recycling.

Recycling Process

Old plastic is taken to a factory and heated until it melts. It is then made into new things such as flower pots, traffic cones, outdoor furniture, and bags. It can also be recycled into polyester fibers, which can be used to make cloth.

Fantastic Fact

Every person throws away about 110 pounds (50 kg) of plastic waste every year. That's enough to make 900 bottles.

27

Glossary

chemicals	tiny substances that join together to make a material, such as plastic or oil
crude oil	thick, black oil that is found in the ground
dye	a strongly colored substance that is used to add color to something
energy	the power that makes machines and living things able to work
environment	all the world around us, including the land, the air, and the sea
experiment	to try out something new
fiber	a long, fine thread
fireproof	unable to be damaged by fire
flexible	bendable
gas	a substance that is neither a liquid nor a solid, like air
granule	a small grain
landfills	places where garbage is buried

mold	a container with a special shape
natural	found in the world around us
oil refinery	a factory where crude oil is made into fuels, plastics, and other materials
pollute	to spoil or poison the air, land, or water with harmful substances
polyester	a synthetic material used to make clothes and other goods
polystyrene	a very light plastic material
recycle	to use an object or material to make something else
synthetic	not natural; made by people
waterproof	not letting water through

Index